Zilch

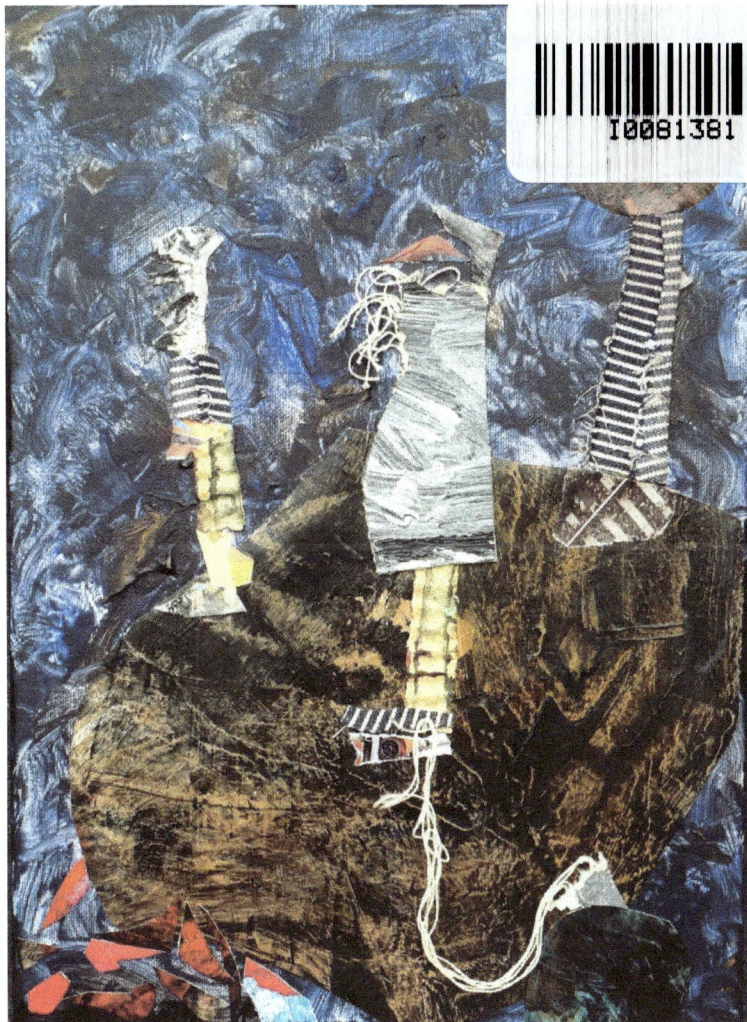

a full-length stage play

Karen Klami

SHIRES ✸ PRESS

Manchester Center, VT 05255

Zilch

a full-length stage play

Printed in the United States of America

Handmaidens (mixed media/acrylic on canvas, 65" x 45")

Rita Fuchsberg
Artist

Cover art & all details from *Departure*
(mixed media on canvas, 16" x 12")

My art is spontaneous and mixed media/acrylic on canvas is my preferred medium. The pieces begin with two flat layers of white gesso and a third layer applied as one would ice a cake. The surface, when dry, has valleys and uneven plains and forms the foundation from which the work will take on a life of its own and accidents are part of the process.

A piece can appear to represent one image and then flip into another. The interpretation is in the eye of the beholder. My heritage informs my imagery. I paint because of an inner necessity to do so.

Several of my works have been exhibited throughout the United States and are part of collections in Africa, Australia and France.

My time is divided between a studio in what my mother calls "a one-horse town" in Vermont, and my hometown, New York City. I live with my shih-tzu, Aurora.

ritadee1127@gmail.com

dedicated

to

my dearest friend

Hasna El Badaoui

and

her wonderful family

who are

an inspiration

to courageous artists

everywhere

who push forward

against

all manner of adversity

in order to create

and share their work

and in doing so

change hearts

and transform lives

Zilch

a full-length play

by

Karen Klami

CHARACTERS:

AMINA AHMED: 18, actress in her father's internationally famous theatre troupe in Morocco. Strong, mature for her age, with an air about her which suggests royalty. She is voluntarily taking on more and more responsibility for the running of her father's theatre since her father has been sick. Fluent in American English, French, and Egyptian Arabic. Her English can make her seem like a native American, but for a small French accent that shows up in certain words now and again.

HARRISON FORD ZILCH: 23, an NYU grad student studying Moroccan culture and doing his thesis on it. Speaks broken Moroccan Arabic and is determined to write a Pulitzer Prize winning "something" in his life. Has been following the Ahmed family's saga and knows a lot about the family.

AREEJ AHMED: 16, actress in same troupe, Amina's younger sister. Has high ambitions to be a famous television star in Egypt and is ready to go whenever the offer is made. Feisty and a little more carefree than Amina. She is the more classically beautiful of the two. Her English is almost flawless American.

ABBAS AHMED (FATHER): 46, founder of the Ahmed Theatre Troupe, famous throughout Morocco and all Northern Africa as a revolutionary theatre group who isn't afraid to criticize the government. Has been diagnosed diabetes which is progressing in small, but potent leaps, because he refuses to take care of himself. But his real problem is a heart condition which he is hiding. Dry humor, feisty, very protective of his daughters. Speaks English with a slight British accent now and again.

NADIR KADAR (MINISTER OF CULTURE): 33, arrogant, yet suave and attractive. Impeccable dresser. Speaks English with a French accent now and again.

JAMILA DAOUD: 18, used to be an actress in the Ahmed Troupe, but has become the Minister of Culture's mistress and gets to work all the time and gets accolades for everything she does, even though is she a greatly inferior to the Ahmed sisters in her talent as an actress. Speaks English with a slight French accent now and again.

<u>SETTING</u>:

Opening scenes are in New York City, dead of winter, at a generic conference center, outside café and an East Village B&B/hotel. The body of play is in Casablanca, Morocco, in various locations. The scenes flow seamlessly, one into the other, using just the suggestion of place and time, created simply with lighting, gobos and sparse, yet specific, set pieces.

<u>TIME</u>:

Present day. Takes place over a one-week period.

NOTE: Live, on-stage, a hand-drumming soloist plays Arabic music, preferably Moroccan folk music rhythms, while scenes change. This may be done when there is no dialogue or when there is a little spoken dialogue as the characters move into the next scene. If possible, one or more Moroccan ethnic instruments can be added.

ACT 1 SCENE 1

AT RISE:
NYC conference room. IN DARKNESS, the dim shape in shadows of AMINA at a podium is outlined by a PowerPoint slide presentation behind her. The last 2-3 slides are shown in silence, and then the lights come. She is apparently finishing a longer presentation. Actors are seated in the audience unknown to the audience. HARRY is one of them.

AMINA

…and so, as you can see from my visual presentation, my home…my dear Morocco…has been enduring a war against its vital life force…its own art! Its own culture!

My father, Abbas Ahmed, the founder of our theatre, has always worked to bring corruption into the light through the power of theatre. He ignites within the people their desire for dignity, social justice, human rights and constructive citizenship. But this present ministry now darkens that light…no, extinguishes it.

Our theatres used to be filled with an audience hungry for our plays. They yearned for someone to speak up for them. But now the Minister of Culture has banned The Ahmed Theatre from the very cities we once made our living.

We suffer exclusion, marginalization and media blackouts because we dare to criticize the corruption which permeates our government. Our unemployed actors are helpless with no monetary means of supporting their families. Some live out on the streets with no protection. They will die destitute, in poverty.

I present to you, here, at the International Arts Conference, a plea for help. Not just for your moral support, but for your financial support, in an arts partnership. Our government limits what we may gain from our European friends. So, my brothers and sisters in countries fighting the same causes, I implore you! Let us finally ban together and create a league to fight this corruption in every corner!

Please join with me to make the Ahmed Theatre once again the beacon for social justice in Morocco…unquenchable and strong. Let us not be extinguished! Thank you.

(AUDIENCE MEMEBERS from the cast clap briefly, begin to get up, but AMINA continues, a bit hurried)

I would like to humbly thank ISPA for giving me this opportunity. Thank you.

(AUDIENCE MEMEBERS while standing clap briefly and leave, talking to one another and say nothing to AMINA. She speaks under her breath)

Nice of you all to show how much you truly care.

(AMINA is packing up her papers as HARRY approaches her slowly and speaks from a distance in the shadows of the audience)

HARRY

I care.

AMINA

(startled, trying to find the source of the voice)
What?

HARRY

(steps into light)
I care.

AMINA

Oh?
(long pause)
That's nice.
(packs papers)

HARRY

They all left and didn't even say a word? Why?

AMINA

And you are…?

HARRY

A secret admirer.

AMINA

Oh, God. That's the worst pick up line I've ever heard. Please. Thanks for listening. But I really...I have to go.

HARRY

Where? Back to your personal hell in Morocco?

AMINA

Great. Look. I don't know you and you're being really rude, so....

HARRY

Why did they just leave without a word? Nothing. That was much, much, much more rude than me. Honestly, don't you think so?

AMINA

Really? You know....they did their duty. They listened politely. Now they will go back to their own difficulties. We're all here to tell our story and try to get help. But there're too many of us in the same predicament. The struggling artists from all these armpits of the world all at once in one room pouring out our hearts and troubles. I shouldn't have bothered to come. Why am I telling you this?

HARRY

But you did come. And I listened. And I care.

AMINA

You already said that. Do you always repeat yourself?

HARRY

Only when provoked by beauty.

AMINA

Who are you?

HARRY

Finally, she wants to know.

AMINA

I already know. Back home you're what we affectionately call "a triple A."

HARRY

Amazing Astounding Artist?

AMINA

No. Annoying Arrogant American.

HARRY

That's New York City for you. Where the sour cream rises to the top.

AMINA

Look, this has been very interesting but I have to catch a plane.

HARRY

No, you don't.

AMINA

I don't think you understand. I'm not interested in your flirtations. Or don't you understand my Moroccan *Muslim woman* accent?

HARRY

I, uh, believe I do since I'm doing my Masters on it. NYU grad student. Doing my thesis on Morocco and how it has shaped the culture of all of Northern Africa for the last century.

AMINA

You astound me.

HARRY

Good. Now it's your turn to astound me over dinner.

AMINA

You're...well, I can't. I have a...

HARRY

...plane to catch. I know. I can see you haven't checked the weather reports. There's a white out. No flights tonight. Major blizzard.

AMINA

That can't be!

HARRY

Check if you want. I already have. I had a flight out tonight that was cancelled. All the airports are shut down until sometime tomorrow.

AMINA

But I already checked out of my hotel!

HARRY

I know a place that has rooms. Downtown. That's where I'm staying. I'll take you there after dinner.

AMINA

I'll find another room.

HARRY

Not at this late hour and not in a blizzard. The hotels are overbooked as it is.

AMINA

I don't know you. I don't trust you.

HARRY
(in Moroccan Arabic)
I am your friend.

AMINA

You are not my friend! You're a stalker! Go away!

HARRY

Ouch! Okay. Suit yourself. But here's my number.
(hands her his card)

9

HARRY (Cont'd)
In case you decide I'm worth the gamble. I think *you* are. Worth it.
> (HARRY walks away as AMINA stands, dumbfounded.
> She awakens from her stupor and checks her cell phone)

AMINA
He's not lying. The airport's closed.
> (reads card)
Harrison Ford Zilch? Sounds fake. Oh, this is just awful.
> (puts card into her pocket, looks up a number on phone
> and dials)
Hello? Hi…I just spent two days at your hotel and checked out this morning. I'd like to get back my room for tonight, please. Well, then any room. I'll pay more for it if... but you...I see. Well, is there any other hotel you can recommend that…? This is New York City! How can every room in every hotel be booked? *You're* sorry? Yeah, good luck to you, too!
> (hangs up)
What a jerk! What a jerk, jerk, jerk, jerk…..jerk…
> (thinking, then takes out card, hesitates, checks some
> more things on phone, stops, looks at card, sighs, then
> dials)
Is this Harrison? This is...yes, it's…yes, I've decided to... What took me so long? You can't be serious. Okay, okay. I'll wait here.
> (hangs up phone)
Be brave, Amina. You've faced worse in Morocco. You are a great actress. You can act your way out of anything…if necessary. And you have a loud whistle and two cans of pepper spray. What can possibly go wrong?
> (pause)
Alright…which way is Mecca?
> (takes a scarf from her bag, contemplates which way is
> Mecca, turns around to face the direction of the audience,
> lays down her coat, kneels down on it, covers her head
> with the scarf, and bows low while softly praying in Arabic.
> LIGHTS DOWN)

10

ACT 1 SCENE 2

Small café, NYC, same night.

> ### AMINA
> No, no! Roger Rabbit is like a cartoon version of a Jimmy Stewart type and Jessica Rabbit was based on Rita Hayworth. Rita Hayworth is my sister's American idol.
>
> ### HARRY
> That's not right. Roger was a kind of mashing together of Bugs Bunny and, I don't know, Robin Williams. And Jessica Rabbit, she's definitely based on Veronica Lake. You know who she is, right?
>
> ### AMINA
> Of course, I do. Haven't we already established I'm extremely well versed in the American golden age of cinema.
>
> ### HARRY
> The hair over one eye. That was her trademark. It's Veronica Lake.
>
> ### AMINA
> No, she didn't have the big hourglass figure. It was Rita Hayworth. The ultimate red-headed male fantasy.
>
> ### HARRY
> Veronica Lake. With a touch of Lauren Bacall. Do you…
>
> ### AMINA
> Yes, I know who she is.
> (Bacall imitation)
> "You know how to whistle, don't you? You just put your lips together and blow."
>
> ### HARRY
> That was an excellent Bacall. However, it is Veronica.

                            AMINA

Rita.

                            HARRY

Veronica.

                            AMINA

Rita it is and the case is closed. I win. Tough luck, kid.

                            HARRY

"Here's looking at you, kid."

                            AMINA

Ah! Yes! My home town. Casablanca. But for me many years
too late. That movie captures the beauty I have never seen.

                            HARRY

That's a downer.

                            AMINA

Sorry.

                            HARRY

Don't be. I'm surprised how much you've been able to survive
and still stay as positive as you are. You're the tough-skinned
one.

                            AMINA

I have to be.

                            HARRY

I know.

                            AMINA

Hmmmm. You know, do you? Know what? What *do* you know?

                            HARRY

Well…I know that you and your sister, Areej, both studied
English through a Christian missionary from Texas. He taught

HARRY (Cont'd)

you to speak English, but with a southern drawl. You speak fluent Moroccan Arabic, Egyptian Arabic, English, French and Spanish. Your father has insisted the family speak English most of the time because he wants you and your sister to be international in scope and influence. Shall I go on?

AMINA

No, please don't. That's what I mean. You scare me. How can you know all that personal information?

HARRY

I haven't even gotten to all we have in common.

AMINA

Why does this part make me shudder the most?

HARRY

Okay, forget it. I'm not out to…just forget it.

AMINA

No. Go ahead.

HARRY

We both know the Arabic speaking world has been the caretaker of the true arts for centuries. And the center of it all is Morocco.

AMINA

No, I don't know that. Why Morocco?

HARRY

It is the Arts Mecca of the Arabic speaking world.
(pause)
Actually, it is *my* center. My father was in the Peace Corp for two years in Tangiers where he fell in love with, Saida…my mother. He'd just finished his masters at Fordham on the popular subject of the influences of the Arabic culture on world culture…or something big and mind-yawning like that. I never understood it, but I appreciate it because that's what made him wander off to Morocco, find my mother, bring her to the States and make me.

HARRY (Cont'd)

Here I am, proof that titanic intellect and insanity can coexist in one human being. I am on a quest to find out if that is due to my American DNA or my Moroccan DNA.

AMINA

Likely due to your Moroccan DNA. Sounds like your father is also titanic.

HARRY

He...was. He died suddenly of an aneurism two months ago.

AMINA

I'm...so sorry.

HARRY

I was obviously going to be the genius man-child. Then my mom became pregnant when I was four, and then lost the baby right after she was born. It was too much for her, I guess. My mother died the next day from some kind of complications.
    (pause)
I remember her eyes. Exotic. And full of kindness.
    (pause)
My father never remarried, but put all his energy into me. I have become the great driven train who lost his engine two months ago. The great Zilch nothing going nowhere.

AMINA

My mother died suddenly in a horrible accident. That was over two years ago. I have nightmares...I... ...but...what about Zilch? That word means nothing, right?

HARRY

You got it.

AMINA

What about the Harrison Ford part of your name.

HARRY

My mother's idea. She was in love with Indiana Jones. You know. The movie.

AMINA

He's a hero.

HARRY

Comic book style. Where's the reality? That's what I'm stuck with now. Reality.

AMINA

You're strong. You've shown a lot of *verve…*
> (pronounces it with a French accent)

Force de vie.

HARRY

Force de stalker. You said so, yourself.

AMINA

I still don't know what you want from me.

HARRY

From you? I…I don't want anything. Well, just maybe for you to like me. Oh, God, I sound like a 13-year-old! That's not too appealing, is it?

AMINA

If you were trying to be appealing you lost me back at Annoying Arrogant American. But you're not.

HARRY

Annoying, arrogant or American?

AMINA

American.

HARRY

Amina…I want to…help you.

AMINA

Do you have a Swiss bank account with a few million dollars?

HARRY

Seriously.

AMINA

Seriously, I am too tired to talk anymore.

HARRY

You must be.

AMINA

I'm sorry. In all our time here I never even said thank you for what you've done, did I?

HARRY

For what?

AMINA

For saving me from spending the night in the airport sleeping on my suitcase. You came to my rescue and I was so rude to you.

HARRY

I'm a dashing knight on Tuesdays, Wednesday and Fridays. You caught me on a good night.
> (pause)

Yes…there is much more to say. But not here. The light's not right and I need mood music.

AMINA

Sometimes I am not sure when to take you seriously.

HARRY

You will discover never is the best policy.
> (holding hand up for the waiter, offstage)

May we have the check?
> (to AMINA)

I hope…I hope you're not uncomfortable with me.

                    AMINA
Too late for both of us, I guess. But you might be growing on
me. Slowly.

                    HARRY
Like a wart.

                    AMINA
Like a wart.

        (LIGHTS DOWN)

ACT 1 SECNE 3

Hallway of hotel, doors to rooms, same night. They wheel in their luggage.

AMINA

This is it.
> (tries the hotel card)

It works.

HARRY

I just wanted to say…I mean, I just thought you were amazing at the conference. They were all idiots.

AMINA

They were tired. I was the last speaker. I should have known better.

HARRY

I don't know how they could not be moved by your presentation.

AMINA

You came in with your own opinions. Agenda.

HARRY

Agenda? That sounds manipulative.

AMINA

I don't mean to sound that way.

HARRY

How do you mean it to sound?
> (getting close to her)

AMINA

Just…honest, maybe.

HARRY
(closer)
Honest? That's not the mark of a suave manipulator and a smooth operator.
(looks as though he is about to embrace her, but wheels around and brings her her suitcase)
I'm much more savvy than that.

AMINA
Much.
(turns and pushes in her luggage)

HARRY
If you need me I'll be down on the second floor with the rest of the peasants.
(starts to leave)

AMINA
Harrison?
(HARRY stops and turns. Long pause)
Will you be my alarm clock?

HARRY
Sure. Of course.

AMINA
My flight is postponed until 2:45 pm. But I want to be up early in the morning and get to the airport. Say about 7:30?

HARRY
Understood.

AMINA
That gives us the day together.

HARRY
It does.

AMINA
When is your flight?

HARRY

Same as yours.

AMINA

Wait. You mean you're on my flight.

HARRY

Yup.

AMINA

You knew this all this time and never said a word.

HARRY

You never asked.

AMINA

And you're staying…

HARRY

In Casablanca at the main hotel. I'm traveling to Marrakesh the day after I arrive.

AMINA

No, you're not.

HARRY

What?

AMINA

You'll stay with us.

HARRY

Amina, you don't have to…

AMINA

My father will be glad to have your company.

HARRY

No, he won't.

AMINA

(smiling)
No, he won't.
(pause)

HARRY

Good night.

AMINA

Good night, Sir Harrison.

(LIGHTS DOWN)

ACT 1 SCENE 4

Airport in Casablanca, next day. AMINA enters with HARRY a few steps behind her. He is pulling both his and her luggage and has had a little trouble with one bag, so he is lagging behind, adjusting the bags. AREEJ enters from one side and runs to AMINA.

                         AREEJ
Amina!
          (they hug)
I can't believe you got to see a snowstorm! I hope I get to see snow like that one day. I was beginning to think maybe you were making excuses because you eloped or something.

                         AMINA
With who? The pilot of the plane?

                         AREEJ
Good choice! But I hear the representative at the conference from Canada was pretty hot.

                         AMINA
How did you even see him?

                         AREEJ
I have my spies everywhere.

                         AMINA
What did you do to your hair?

                         AREEJ
I used henna. Like it?

                         AMINA
No! Not really, no.

AREEJ

I want to be different from all the other black-haired, slick, boring, wanna-be princesses. I'm Areej Ahmed! The Bright Red Flame of Safar! The Rita Hayworth of Alexandria and Cairo!

AMINA

You're still in Casablanca, little girl.

HARRY

(coming up from behind, wheeling the luggage)
You do actually know who Rita Hayworth is.

(AREEJ wheels around to encounter HARRY, who she looks up and down)

AREEJ

So, you fell for the bellboy?

HARRY

Pleased to meet the Flame.
(HARRY bows)

AREEJ

(to AMINA)
I can see why you dragged him along. He's definitely better than the Canadian.
(to HARRY)
And to answer your question, I am very fond of old Hollywood movies. Are you surprised? Everything American, old and new, is very big here.
(to AMINA)
He's adorable. Where did you...?

AMINA

It's a long story and I'm really tired and want to go home.
(ABBAS hurriedly walks in and goes straight to AMINA and gives her a great big bear hug, not taking note of HARRY. AREEJ continues to eye HARRY)
Baba! What are you doing here? Where is Tariq? I thought he'd be picking me up.

ABBAS

He was busy. I have his car. We should hurry. Where are your
bags?
    (AMINA gestures toward HARRY who is beaming with a
    smile)
What is this?

AREEJ

"Who is this" would be the proper English, Baba.

HARRY

    (in Arabic, but using the word "warrior" instead of
    "director")
I am very pleased to meet the great warrior, Abbas Ahmed.
    (AREEJ bursts out laughing, AMINA hides her laugh, and
    ABBAS looks at HARRY and then at AMINA)

AMINA

    (to HARRY)
You said great "warrior." I don't think you meant…

HARRY

Oh…oh. Yea. I'm sorry.

ABBAS

I have to say, that has to be the first time I have ever been called
a warrior, but I like it. Who are you, young man?

HARRY

My name is…

AMINA

I'd like to explain about him. He's…

ABBAS

    (looks around nervously)
Not here. Where is he going?
    (to HARRY)
Where are you going?

ABBAS (Cont'd)
(before HARRY can answer)
I can drive you. We can talk on the way.
(starts to push them off in one direction)

AMINA
Why are you in so much of a hurry?

AREEJ
(under her breath)
Don't ask questions. Just move, okay?

AMINA
He's staying with us.
(ABBAS stops abruptly)
He's…a friend. An American friend.

ABBAS
Oh, that's just wonderful! My daughter goes to America and somehow manages in that short time to pick up a wide-eyed American tourist who saw a television special about exotic Morocco and wants to "experience" it first hand while living with the charming indigenous people!

AMINA
Baba!

HARRY
I can understand your doubts and concerns about Americans. But I can assure you, sir, I am not what you think I am.

AMINA
He's not.

AREEJ
I hope he's not.

HARRY
I'm not.

ABBAS
(pauses and looks HARRY up and down)
I hate the way Americans dress. Blue jeans. They think they
look so chic if they wear them with that one style shirt they saw in
the "Sexiest Man Alive" issue of Esquire. You can dress up a
donkey like a show horse, but underneath, he's still a jackass.

AREEJ
(to HARRY)
You're growing on him. He likes you.

ABBAS
(nervously looking around)
We have to go. Bring him along. He can take the bags.

HARRY
Of course.

(ABBAS exists first, followed by AMINA, followed by
HARRY, with AREEJ smiling, never taking her eyes off
HARRY. LIGHTS DOWN)

ACT 1 SCENE 5

Ahmed home, next morning. Sound of call to prayer. HARRY enters room, looking out the window. It is sunrise. Lights are very low and start to come up slowly as he listens to the call to prayer. AMINA enters and watches HARRY, unnoticed. He sees her as then lights come up more quickly to brighter sunlight. Call to prayer ends.

HARRY

My father used to talk about this all the time. He'd play videos of this so I could see and hear it. He said it was one of the most sublime things he'd ever experienced when he first arrived in Morocco and it changed him forever. Now I know why.

AMINA

I'll take you to the Hassan II Mosque. There you stand on the sea to pray. The minaret is the 13th largest in the world. It has 41 fountains, a beautiful courtyard, a garden…

AREEJ

(entering with a jilaba)

You both sound like a travelogue. Good morning, Harrison.

HARRY

Ah, the red-head fire-goddess. Good morning, Areej. Yes, I know about the mosque. It's pretty famous.

AMINA

I'd like to take you there so you can see it through the eyes of one from Casablanca.

HARRY

Through your eyes, then. Yes, I'd like that. Prayerful eyes?

AMINA

More like hopeful eyes.

AREEJ
When I get my superstar leading roles on Egyptian television, I will change my name to Fire Goddess of Safar.
>(hands HARRY the jilaba)

My father thought you might want this.
>(HARRY holds it puzzled)

It's a jilaba.
>(pause)

You wear it.
>(AREEJ begins to prepare Moroccan tea and some cakes with honey. She and AMINA will serve them throughout the scene)

AMINA
He doesn't need that. He can wear his own western clothing. It'll make him look like a tourist.

HARRY
I'd be honored if he wants me to wear it.

AMINA
You don't have to.

AREEJ
I would, if I were you.

AMINA
He doesn't have to conform to us. He's allowed to be himself. We wear western clothes. Why should he wear it?

HARRY
I'm half Moroccan. I'd like to.

AMINA
I wish you wouldn't.

HARRY
But if your father wants me to.

                    AMINA
He is not the ruler over you!

                    AREEJ
Amina!

                    HARRY
But I am a guest in his house.

                    AMINA
Because I insisted you be!

        (ABBAS enters)

                    ABBAS
But I gave *my* permission. Harrison, you don't have to wear it,
but from our conversation in the car last night, I thought you
might wish to. You are half one of us.

                    HARRY
Thank you, sir.

                    ABBAS
Sir? I am surprised and delighted you are sincerely a polite
American. That has not been my common experience. You
fooled me…Mr.
        (says each part of his name slowly)
Harrison…Ford…Zilch. What does it mean?

                    HARRY
Mean?

                    ABBAS
What does your name mean?

                    AMINA
Nothing.

                    ABBAS
It has to mean something.

31

HARRY

The Harrison Ford part is from the movie.
        (ABBAS gives a blank look)
Indiana Jones? Harrison Ford is the actor who plays him?
        (ABBAS gives a blank look)
He's very famous in America. And Zilch. That's a word that literally means "nothing."

ABBAS

You need a better name.

HARRY

The story of my life.

ABBAS

Well, you aren't one of "them." Those "triple A's." Arrogant Annoying…

HARRY

Yes, Amina told me.

ABBAS

At least my instincts tell me you're not and I rely heavily on my instincts.
        (sipping tea)
I didn't think it was a good idea for Amina to go to New York City. She was elected as an International Young Leader. It was a great honor and she was invited to speak. They paid for everything. I thought she should experience the USA. It would put a perspective on her life. But her meeting someone like you was one of my deepest fears. Hooked by the American lifestyle. Seduced by an American gold-digger!
        (starts eating many pieces of cake)

AREEJ

Gold-digger? That's the name for women who look for rich men. Wait! Was Harrison seduced by my sister, an exotic Moroccan heiress? Sorry to disappoint you, but we're not rich! Are you?

HARRY
Not in the ways you mean.

AREEJ
Baba! You're eating too many of them. Your blood sugar will go through the roof!
>(ABBAS stuffs a big cake with honey into his mouth and smiles)

AMINA
That's not funny!
>(taking away the tray)

ABBAS
Leave it! I am not a child!
>(AMINA reluctantly puts it back)

They don't realize that if I am going to die soon, I'd like it to be with a full belly of my favorite cakes.

HARRY
I just want to tell you, Mr. Ahmed, Sir, that Amina was brilliant at the conference. Her presentation and speech were top quality and very moving.

ABBAS
Did it get anyone to commit to helping us?

AMINA
Not yet.

ABBAS
Then it seems it was received like a hot air balloon that is puffed up and flies high but does not persuade. Does not impress.

HARRY
She was very impressive! She was amazing! She…

AREEJ
More tea, Harrison?
>(gives him a look as if to say, "Don't challenge.")

ABBAS

I am not speaking of failure. Amina attempted to open a window into the minds of those at the conference and show them what we are fighting for…and against. But the choice of aiding us is always theirs. It isn't emotion you want, but a commitment of the mind.

HARRY

I have been studying the Ahmed family's theatre troupe for quite a while and I…

AMINA

Harrison is very accomplished. He is working on his masters at NYU. His thesis is on Morocco and how it has shaped the culture of North Africa. He is looking to interview you to talk about it.

ABBAS

Me? Ha! What can I say to an NYU student that he doesn't already believe he knows?

HARRY

I have so much to ask you about your theatre and what you've done for Morocco.

ABBAS

What we've done? The Ahmeds are very sneaky. We have stolen from the greats, have made it our own, and in this way have avoided being arrested and put in jail for years. We have ignited revolution without them ever finding the source of the fire.

HARRY

And how have you done this?

ABBAS

We don't talk about family secrets. It would spoil everything. And now I must go to see *our* distinguished Minister of Culture, the illustrious Mr. Kadar.

                              AMINA
That's not even close to funny. But why so early? I'm going with
you.

                              ABBAS
Not for this meeting. I have something…that needs special
attention. I won't be long.

                              AREEJ
I'll call Tariq for his car?

                              ABBAS
Yes, he knows. Tell him to be out front in half an hour. Well,
Harrison Ford Zilch. I'll need to get to know you more before I
can give you a proper name. If you're going to stay in my house,
you're going to have to be more than "nothing."

                              HARRY
Thank you, sir.

                              ABBAS
Sir. Ha! I love it.
          (While AMINA and AREEJ are not looking, ABBAS grabs
          a cake off the tray and exits. AREEJ picks up a cell
          phone and walks off, making the call)

                              AMINA
He's…sometimes he makes me…he's so stubborn and he…

                              HARRY
He loves you more than you will ever understand. I can see it.

                              AMINA
But I will never really please him.

                              HARRY
Why didn't you speak up? Say something when he said you
didn't succeed?

AMINA

Because, as usual, he's right. I didn't. And you don't cross examine my father. You'll learn.

HARRY

I have a fantastic idea. Take me to that amazing Hassan II Mosque. I want to stand on the sea and pray.

AMINA

Alright.

HARRY

But first...I want to put on my tourist jilaba.
(starts to exit, AMINA follows)

AMINA

No, you don't! No, please! You don't really want you to do that! Harrison!

(LIGHTS DOWN)

ACT 1 SCENE 6

Outside the main Casablanca TV Station, same day. Sign with insignia for this station which says, "SNRT TV: Société Nationale de Radiodiffusion et de Télévison." HARRY is standing outside of the station waiting for AMINA. He is in his normal clothing, and holding some street vendor food, which is something like a b'stilla (pastry with layers of paper-thin pastry stuffed with meat and spices) and orange juice. JAMILA comes out of the building, sees HARRY, but he doesn't see her. He is trying to balance the food and eat it without dropping it. Finally, he does drop it. JAMILA speaks from where she is.

                    JAMILA
Oh, that's a shame. It looked like a delicious b'stilla.
          (HARRY turns around, dropping the rest)

                    HARRY
It was.

                    JAMILA
They make the best ones near the great mosque. Hassan II's Mosque.

                    HARRY
That's where I got it. Was just there a while ago. Beautiful.

                    JAMILA
Then double the shame it has been lost.
          (JAMILA moves to HARRY)
British?

                    HARRY
American.

                    JAMILA
Your accent is…?

                    HARRY
New York.

                    JAMILA
Ah.

                    HARRY
I've worked on it all my life so it wouldn't be so obvious, but I
guess I can't hide it here.

                    JAMILA
No, it would be hard to hide *you* here. I think you are not one
anyone one would wish to hide, except maybe for themselves.

                    HARRY
Thank you…I think.

                    JAMILA
Are you an actor for radio or television?

                    HARRY
No.

                    JAMILA
A producer? Director?

                    HARRY
No.

                    JAMILA
Lost tourist, then?

                    HARRY
Eh, no.

                    JAMILA
Then why are you eating outside our station?

                    HARRY
Oh, I'm waiting for someone. Amina Ahmed. Do you know her?

JAMILA

Everyone knows her. She's from the famous Ahmeds of the Theatre. How do you know her?

HARRY

I followed her here from America.

JAMILA

Really? That's a long way to come. Why would you come here for her?

HARRY

That's a long story. We are friends. I am staying at her house.

JAMILA

Really? How strange Abbas would let you stay there.

HARRY

I…I didn't quite catch your name.

JAMILA

Jamila. Jamila Daoud.
        (HARRY extends his hand to hers and they shake)

HARRY

Harrison Ford Zilch.

JAMILA

Comical name.

HARRY

Thanks. I laugh every time I say it.

JAMILA

I offend you.

HARRY

No, not really.

                              JAMILA

I did. I am sorry.

                              HARRY

It's nothing.

                              JAMILA

        (approaches him)
Can I make it up to you?

                              HARRY

How?

                              JAMILA

I work for the Minister of Culture. I'm an actress. I work here all
the time. Do you wish to do something here at the station?
        (walks around him, like she is studying a sculpture)

                              HARRY

Me? No. I'm more interested in traditional Moroccan culture and
linguistics. I'm doing my master's thesis on it. I'm…

                              JAMILA

You're a student? You're too old to be one.

                              HARRY

I'm a graduate student.

                              JAMILA

I can help you with anything you want. I have many connections.
I can help you see people you can't see.

                              HARRY

Why? Why do you want to help me? You don't even know me.

                              JAMILA

You're a friend of Amina Ahmed. We used to work together in
her father's theatre. But no more. Her father was very kind to
me. I'd like to show my respects to him by helping a friend of his.

HARRY

A friend of *hers.* I'm *Amina's* friend.

JAMILA

So, you are…for now. Do you want my help?

HARRY

I'm not sure.

JAMILA

Just come here and ask for me by name. I'll help you with anything you want. Well, ta for now. Au revoir, l'homme délicieux.
> (she exits)

HARRY

Au revoir.
> (fans himself)

Delicious man? I knew it'd be hot in Morocco, but not this kind of hot.
> (busies himself trying to clean up the mess of the pastry on the ground. AMINA enters)

AMINA

You still praying?

HARRY

What? No. No, I dropped it.

AMINA

Quel damage. I really wanted that.

HARRY

Sorry. I just met someone who says they can help me with my thesis. She works for the Ministry.

AMINA

She? What does she look like?

HARRY

A lot like you, except, well, not as pretty, but she…

AMINA

What's her name?

HARRY

Jamila Daoud.

AMINA

Oh, great.

HARRY

What's the matter?

AMINA

You just got hit on, didn't you?

HARRY

Yeah, I guess you can call it that. But it was really weird.

AMINA

That's the Minister of Culture's mistress. She's a top actress in shows approved by the Ministry. She has work all the time. An apartment, a salary, a pension, health care. And she's "provided for," if you know what I mean.

HARRY

Really? She seems very young.

AMINA

That's the way he likes them.

HARRY

She said she was an actress in your troupe.

AMINA

She was. She was a huge…problem. Before she…do we have to talk about her?

                    HARRY

Not if it upsets you.

                    AMINA

She doesn't. It's them, in there. They are Nadir's puppets and I
am sick of it.

                    HARRY

Nadir?

                    AMINA

Nadir Kadar. Minister of Culture. Minister of Death. Minister of
Bribes. Minister of…

                    HARRY

I think I get it.

                    AMINA

They cancelled our third season!

                    HARRY

What does that mean?

                    AMINA

It means it is getting easier and easier for him to make it worse
and worse for us. We signed a three-season contract with this
station and did the first two seasons. It was our original special
TV show. I wrote most of the episodes with Areej. It's called
"Vivre Vivant," … "Living Alive."

                    HARRY

As opposed to living dead?

                    AMINA

Precisely! Living with your eyes open to what is happening
around you. Living a life full of passion for doing what is right.
Of course, it challenged the political authorities, too. We always
sneak that in there.

HARRY

Of course.

AMINA

We wrote the show in French to get it approved and produced
here, but when we filmed it, we did it in Arabic, so that the people
would understand it so we could reach many. It was an
enormous success. We were extremely popular. But that's what
killed us. Our great popularity. Now they are refusing to give us
a permit to film our third contracted season.

HARRY

I'm so sorry.

AMINA

It was our last way to earn money for this year. I don't know
what to do. Nadir and his great jealousy. I wonder if that is what
my father was going to see him about? But there is no reasoning
with him.

HARRY

This might sound strange, but do you think Jamila might help.

AMINA

I just told you she is his mistress. Why would she help?

HARRY

Just a feeling.

AMINA

She beguiled you. She does that. She always has…an effect on
men.

HARRY

That she does.

AMINA

Is that a rocket in your pocket or were you just happy to see her?

HARRY

That's cruel, Amina.

AMINA

You're right. I'm sorry, and...I need to go home and...try to think...

HARRY

Maybe your father has already fixed it when he met with the Minister?
(AREEJ arrives, out of breath)

AREEJ

I found you! Oh, God! I've been running everywhere looking for you!

AMINA

What is it?

AREEJ

Baba is in hospital. He collapsed outside of Nadir's office. I told him not to eat those cakes. I told him...
(AREEJ starts to cry. HARRY comforts her)

AMINA

It's diabetic shock. It's happened before. He'll be alright.

HARRY

How far is it?

AMINA

Not far. I'll meet you there.
(AREEJ nods and starts to go)
Harrison, please go with Areej. I have someone to see first.

HARRY

I don't think that's a good idea.

AMINA

Can you suggest a better plan?

45

> HARRY

Be careful.

> AMINA

That's how I got this far.

> HARRY

You're magnificent.
> (HARRY runs off after AREEJ)

Areej! Wait! I'm coming with you.

> AMINA

Allah be praised, I will win this battle for you, Baba.

> (LIGHTS DOWN)

ACT 1 SCENE 7

Hospital in Casablanca, same afternoon. HARRY and AREEJ
are beside ABBAS sitting in a wheelchair.

                    ABBAS
No flowers? Isn't it an American tradition to visit someone in
hospital with flowers?

                    AREEJ
You have allergies.

                    ABBAS
He doesn't know that.

                    HARRY
I apologize. I'll come with flowers tomorrow.

                    AREEJ
          (adjusting ABBAS' blankets and pillow)
Are you comfortable?

                    ABBAS
Do I look like I am? Where is my hookah?

                    AREEJ
     (to HARRY)
He doesn't smoke. He'll have to settle for flowers that will make
him sneeze.

                    ABBAS
You are just too good to me daughter number two.

                    AREEJ
I try.

                    HARRY
You look much better.

47

ABBAS

(to AREEJ)
He doesn't lie very well. Good trait to be a lousy liar.

AREEJ

Did they give you insulin?

ABBAS

No, they gave me an ice cream cone in the form of a drip.
Vanilla.

AREEJ

(to HARRY)
I'll check with the nurse what he needs.
(AREEJ exits)

ABBAS

I like to keep the atmosphere light.

HARRY

I'm not sure that was working.

ABBAS

I'm just warming up. I get better for the evening show.
(AREEJ returns)
She's back to torment me already?

AREEJ

The nurse says she will be coming around to check on you and
that right now you are supposed to be sleeping. She's surprised
the medication hasn't hit you yet.

HARRY

I think it's best we let you sleep.

ABBAS

I am getting a little sleepy. I miss my tea. Bring me tea. Sneak
it in. Now I'm an old man who needs a nap.
(he starts to nod off, but fights it)

48

AREEJ
(to HARRY)
He gets more difficult each day.

ABBAS
(pushing against sleep)
I can hear you talk about me…you're making…me…feel like I
don't exist anymore….
(ABBAS nods off. AREEJ takes HARRY to the side)

AREEJ
I've been wanting to talk to you all day. He's been acting really
weird since just before Amina came back.

HARRY
Is it because he's sick?

AREEJ
No. No. He insisted on going to the airport to pick up Amina.
He wasn't supposed to. He actually looked, I don't know.
Frightened. All my life I saw my father go to jail many times
because of his political theatre. But I never saw fear in his face.
There is something up he's not telling us.

ABBAS
(half awakening)
Where is Amina?

AREEJ
Fixing things.

ABBAS
Tell her I want her here. Tell her she must come here now.

AREEJ
What's the matter, Baba?

ABBAS
Nothing but your horrible red hair!
(waking up more)

AREEJ
It has given me my new name. I love my new name. Fire Goddess!

ABBAS
Your name is Areej and it means a pleasant smell. A visionary.

AREEJ
Then I envision myself dripping with furs, smelling very pleasant, while I'm the star of my own television series.

HARRY
Stop dreaming so small, Areej.

ABBAS
And now for you. Your name is now Munjid. It means "rescuer."

HARRY
I think that may be a little too much for me to take on.

AREEJ
Baba. I can phone Amina. She can…

ABBAS
Go! Go, go, go!
    (AREEJ exits. ABBAS and HARRY are alone)
I heard what she said. I was just acting like I was sleeping. Fooled you, huh, great actor that I am. She shouldn't worry about me.

HARRY
Do you blame her for worrying?

ABBAS
She's the loud and stubborn part of her mother. But Amina…she's a perfect copy of my Amira. Gone, you know. Two years next month.

HARRY

I know about the tragedy.

ABBAS

They said she didn't feel a thing because the train that hit her was going so fast the impact must have killed her instantly. I like to think there was no pain.
(pause)
When she was gone, I gave over my devotion to my King. All these years he's tolerated me and why? Because in all my screaming about injustice and corruption I weed out for him all the bad fruit he can't see. But now he's given it all away to a bastard son. The irony. My theatre is responsible for many lives. Now the Ministry won't hire any of them because they worked for me. They suffer because of loyalty.

HARRY

They should be proud to have been with you and not with that devil.

ABBAS

Speaking of the devil, my poor little Areej wants to run off to the devil's city. She has no idea what she will have to do to make it in Egypt.

HARRY

She shouldn't go.

ABBAS

But she will. Maybe it is right for her to fly away like the bird she is. What's here for her now?
(pause)
It's my heart, you know. Not the diabetes. A valve or two not working. That's what's causing all my real problems. That's truly a joke on me. I have always made sure my art touched the mind and *not* the heart. The heart is the enemy because it changes with emotions. The deepest, unchanging convictions happen in the mind.

                              HARRY

She's strong in both.

                              ABBAS

What?

                              HARRY

Amina. She's got a strong heart and mind.

                              ABBAS

That's my worry. She doesn't really know which one to follow.
        (tries to get up, but can't)
I'm sorry you are here at this time. I was always a raging bull.
Now look at me. Maybe you should take Amina away from here.

                              HARRY

No…no, that's not why I came.

                              ABBAS

She's killing herself trying to make it all right. And she thinks the
theatre is all I really care about. Not her.

                              HARRY

She's amazingly strong.

                              ABBAS

That's just a disguise. I taught her that. I can see right through
it. And I also see you actually do truly love her.

                              HARRY

Sir, I…we just met.

                              ABBAS

There's that "sir" thing again. Forget everything you ever learned
at the NYU school and lean on what you know now. What really
brought you here?

                              HARRY

I thought it was my thesis.

ABBAS

Wrong.

HARRY

I knew all my studies of your family weren't just this academic zeal inside me. And not just a stupid attempt to please my father. Of course. Amina.

ABBAS

Careful though. She's a tough puzzle like her mother. Exactly…like her…

(ABBAS is having trouble breathing, clutching his chest)

Call…the nurse…

HARRY

Sir?

(goes to him)

Oh, my God!

(yelling)

Nurse! Nurse!

(goes to doorway and yells)

Infirmière! Ici!! Ici!!

(ABBAS is having a heart attack. LIGHTS DOWN)

ACT 1 SCENE 8

Nadir's office at the Ministry, same afternoon. Lights up on NADIR'S office. He is standing with some papers as AMINA rushes in.

AMINA
(in Arabic)
You knew exactly what you were doing blocking our contract with the station. How dare you?

NADIR
And good afternoon to you, too, Miss Ahmed. Nice of you to drop in and express yourself so eloquently. But please. Speak English. I want to practice my diction.

AMINA
We had a signed contract for three seasons. They would never break it unless they received direct instructions from the Minister of Culture. What did you promise them in return?

NADIR
I didn't tell them to do anything. If they dropped you, that was their choice.

AMINA
After you bought them with favors.

NADIR
I'd be careful how you phrase your accusations.

AMINA
Is that what my father came to see you about this morning?

NADIR
That, my sweet, is between me and your father.

AMINA
I don't like games, Nadir.

NADIR

Neither do I. We've known each other since you were 10 and I was…

AMINA

A grown man of 25 looking for a child to play with.

NADIR

I don't believe you were ever a child, Amina. You have always been a woman since you came out of the womb. A very appealing one.

AMINA

We needed that contract. We have no work. No permits. No prospects for income. And we employ others who need the work. Or are you forgetting that, too?

NADIR

That's show business, my dear. But why isn't your father traveling to his faithful followers abroad for money?

AMINA

There are no followers abroad. Not anymore. And his diabetes makes him weak. Just now he took sick and is in hospital. Right after he saw you.

NADIR

That's unfortunate. But I had nothing to do with the station. They are setting up a new season featuring more French-based material. They probably felt your traditional series was too old-fashioned.

AMINA

We were their biggest success! The people love us!

NADIR

They're changing with the current. You know, you should really try to do something current, Amina. Look at you. You are extremely attractive. Jamila doesn't hold a candle to you.

NADIR (Cont'd)
(moves to her, stroking her with the papers in his hand)
You could have been right here, in Jamila's shoes. Having what she has. And you, with so much more talent.

AMINA
You disgust me. A married man and you carry on like this in the open.

NADIR
You have no filter on you. Like your father. Haven't you heard? It's a perk of western culture to have a mistress. Or aren't you aware of how westernization has benefited us Moroccans?
(mockingly patriotic)
Viva la France!

AMINA
Enslaved us, you mean. Colonialism is alive again, living inside your Ministry. Only this time as *willing* slaves because you pay them off.

NADIR
Slaves? You are freed from all restraints. No forced wearing of the hijab. No curfew. Free!

AMINA
What you and I call freedom are very different.

NADIR
Let's get past all the animosity. Like that word? My English is getting so much better, isn't it? Sit down, Amina, so we can talk like old friends.
(AMINA remains standing)
I hear you have an American visitor. Oh, don't look so surprised. Jamila told me. I think she was taken with him. He's here for…?

AMINA
He's a student.

NADIR

A little old for arithmetic lessons.

AMINA

He's doing his thesis on Morocco.

NADIR

And you just found him by chance in New York City? Was he sitting, destitute, in the gutter like a stray puppy and you took him in?

AMINA

Nadir…

NADIR

(suddenly explosive)

Who do you think you are coming in here and talking to me as if I were your equal? You flaunt your so-called virtue at us as if we should bow down in worship. The Holy Abbas and his virgin daughters. What do you expect?

(JAMILA has entered, unseen, and stays in the shadows while he talks)

We laugh at you, you and your false morality. If I want to have my mistress or anyone I wish, that's what I am free to do. I will not let you infect us with your version of right or wrong or corrupt or pure!

(pause)

Oh, Amina Ahmed! You see how you rile me up? What an effect you have always had on me? Teasing me? See what you do to me?

AMINA

I see very well. But what *you* don't see is…we will win. You can't stop us.

(JAMILA enters and makes herself seen)

NADIR

Jamila? What is it?

JAMILA

It's…important.

NADIR

Not now.
      (AREEJ suddenly enters, looking around to find AMINA,
      with HARRY and JAMILA behind him)

AMINA

Areej?

AREEJ

      (she goes directly to AMINA and hugs her)
Baba's had a heart attack.
      (AMINA pushes AREEJ away)
He's in a coma.
      (AMINA shakes herself out of momentary shock, then
      quickly exits, without a word, followed by AREEJ. JAMILA
      stands aside. HARRY looks at her, then at NADIR, then
      is about to exit. NADIR steps in front of him)

NADIR

So, you must be the stray puppy from America. Amina's told me
all about you. I'm Nadir Kadar, Minister of Culture.
      (extends his hand for a shake. HARRY looks at it, then
      looks at him)

HARRY

Go to hell.
      (HARRY exits)

NADIR

Charming.
      (turns to JAMILA)
Come here. Don't look so sad.
      (JAMILA reluctantly goes to NADIR. He moves behind
      her, stroking her neck, but she seems frozen)
It's alright. Baba Abbas will be okay. I know how you love him
like a father.

59

NADIR (Cont'd)
(he kisses her neck)
I want *you* so bad. My Jamila.
(she stands motionless. He continues to kiss her neck
from behind. LIGHTS DOWN)

END OF ACT 1

ACT 2 SCENE 1

Ahmed home, next morning. Areej is packing.

AMINA
This isn't the best time for you to be leaving.

AREEJ
Not the best time? Can you actually think of a better time? We need the money now. I'll be sending back much more in one week than you can make here in a month.

AMINA
If you can get the work.

HARRY
How do you know you will get it?

AMINA
She doesn't.

AREEJ
I'll stay with Lateefah. She's been wanting me to come. Husani will find me something.

AMINA
You can't trust that Husani will be able to get you work right away. So far this has only been a dream, but now you have to look at the reality. Remember what happened to Karima? She was nearly raped by that producer, and when she refused him, she was forced to leave her show.

AREEJ
And she survived very well. She was on the show just long enough to gain fame. Another show hired her right away. Now she's doing even better.

AMINA
I don't want you hurt.

AREEJ
Do you think I'm not already hurting right here?

AMINA
You'll be thrown into situations there I don't want to see you in.
I'm afraid, Areej.

AREEJ
Look, Husani can get me something small right away. I'm sure
of it. It'd just be a start but at least it would be something. Here
we have…nothing.

AMINA
Can't you just wait a bit longer? Until Baba is a little better?

> (AREEJ and HARRY are silent. The elephant in the room
> is that they know he won't get better)

AREEJ
Amina. Please. I have to do this.

HARRY
I think maybe she does.

AREEJ
No matter what I get, at least I won't have to lower myself to that
horrible French mockery we have here. They have their own
style in Egypt. It's not trés chic but at least it's *not* trés French!
I'm tired of us being the "Niggers of Arabia."

HARRY
The what?

AMINA
We are portrayed as the "Niggers of the French Colonialists," still
today, years after our independence.

HARRY
I think there might be a better way to say that.

AMINA

Is there a better way to say being made a mockery of in the most disgusting ways?

AREEJ

It's not like that in Egypt.

AMINA

It's worse in *other* ways.

AREEJ
(does a funny face and dances around like an ape, speaking in Arabic)
Look at my ugly, dumb, uneducated Moroccan face! We are all so happy even though we are so dirty and smell like onions and piss!
(she does a prat fall and writhes on the ground, then gets up and continues to pack)

HARRY

I think I got some of that. Something about happy Moroccans with ugly faces and smelling like...piss?

AREEJ

Ugly, dumb, uneducated, dirty. All the government sanctioned shows do that.

AMINA

The French copy the Americans sitcom style, but very badly. The Moroccans copy the French, also badly, making fun of their own people. The actors all say that when working for the government shows they are humiliated because they are humiliating their own people. But they get paid well. They put it all aside to survive.

AREEJ

They have no writers but just improvise on those bad scenarios they get from France. Boring sitcoms. Cheap laughs. All at our expense.

AMINA
We are *Le Petite Moroccan*. Tiny little criminals, drug addicts, beating our wives. And what's the best part is that the Minister of Culture gets paid well for buying the French scenarios.

HARRY
And so French Colonialism is alive and well.

AREEJ
And that's why I have to get out of here.
> (has packed one bag and puts it aside, picks up her phone and dials)

It won't be for a couple of days. I've still got paperwork to do. I'll visit Baba at hospital every day until I leave. Amina, I…
> (embraces AMINA, then pulls away, and talks into the phone)

Hello? Hello! Lateefah! It's Areej! Yes. I have bad *and* good news…
> (speaks in Arabic as she exits)

HARRY
I think I am beginning to understand just what an Ahmed is made of.

AMINA
What's that?

HARRY
Pure steel.

AMINA
I wouldn't be so sure.
> (pause)

I have something I want to show you. Come…
> (AMINA takes HARRY by the hand and they exit, as it flows into the next scene without a blackout)

ACT 2 SCENE 2

At the abandoned theatre, the Ahmed Theatre House of
Casablanca, the same day. Amina takes Harry to the theatre
where they have performed for years, but no longer.

HARRY

What is this place?

AMINA

Our old theatre. The famous Ahmed Theatre House of
Casablanca.

HARRY

It looks like a palace.

AMINA

It was for us. We had this theatre for many years. I grew up
doing all my father's shows in here. When they needed children
in the plays, I got all those roles. I was a little starlet. Very
obnoxious. Even more than my sister, if you can believe it. All
right in here.
> (moves around the room, then onto an area which would
> have been the stage. HARRY claps)

HARRY

Good acoustics.
> (gets up on the stage)
"To be or not to be, that is the question."

AMINA

"Whether 'tis nobler in the mind to suffer
The slings and arrows of outrageous fortune,
Or to take arms against a sea of troubles
And by opposing end them. To die—to sleep,
No more…"
> (pause)
I forget the rest.

HARRY

Shakespeare. You're the Hamlet of Morocco.

AMINA

I've always identified with him. Still do.

HARRY

I think anyone who has ever thought about ending it all has. But not you. Not you.

AMINA

You make too many assumptions, Mr. Harrison Ford Zilch. It will be your downfall.

HARRY

I have many other faults to help that along.

AMINA

I've always been so focused on being the champion of my father's theatre. But when I try to focus on myself, I get lost.

HARRY

I don't think he wants you to be the champion of his theatre. I think he wants you to find yourself.

AMINA

You don't know my father.

HARRY

I'm not sure you do.
    (pause)
How do you know Hamlet so well?

AMINA

No actor is worth his or her salt who can't quote Hamlet.

HARRY

I wouldn't know.

                          AMINA
I grew up with all the classics. That's the family secret.

                          HARRY
What is?

                          AMINA
What my father wouldn't tell you. How he stopped getting
arrested all the time.
        (pause, with HARRY still puzzled)
My father took the classics and he *adapted* them. Brecht.
Volpone. Molière. Strindberg. The government officials didn't
know the stories, so when they came to arrest him for exposing
corruption or complaining about the lack of workers' rights he'd
just say, "I'm only doing the play *as written*." They could do
nothing. Survival by being clever.

                          HARRY
Survival by being clever.

                          AMINA
But that's all over. Now there is…

                          HARRY
Zilch.

                          AMINA
What?

                          HARRY
I think I've jinxed your family.

                          AMINA
What? That's crazy.

                          HARRY
Ever since I came back with you there has been nothing but
endless troubles for you all. And I feel so helpless. I can't do
anything.

                              AMINA

You're doing a lot for me.

                              HARRY

Do I?

                              AMINA

I'm not sure I could get through this without you.

                              HARRY

It's hard for me to hear that. I mean, the way you dissed me at
the conference.

                              AMINA

I was angry then. No one was listening and I was so desperate.
That's a lifetime ago. Now…now I'm terrified.

                              HARRY

Do you believe in love at first sight?

                              AMINA

Oh, come on! Another corny line. Just when I thought you'd
grown out of them. This isn't Romeo and Juliet!

                              HARRY

I know, and yet…

                              AMINA

That's just silly nonsense and dreamy, drivel.

                              HARRY

Then that's what I am. Dreamy drivel. And that's what you are.
Because I adore you, Amina.

                              AMINA

That's not funny. Stop it.
          (HARRY kisses her. She laughs)

                              HARRY

That's not exactly the reaction I was hoping for.

                    AMINA
Wait. I mean. Wait. Are you…

                    HARRY
Serious? Yes, this is the first time I am going to say take me
seriously. Because…I've wanted you so much…because…
          (kisses her)
I'm…
          (kisses her)
Completely…
          (pulls her very close)
Head over heels…
          (kisses her again and she reciprocates in a big way. They
          kiss and become very passionate. It has become a lot
          more passionate than either of them expected. They lay
          down on the stage and HARRY is on top of her. They are
          fully clothed. HARRY starts to undress her and she isn't
          stopping it for a while)

                    AMINA
          (softly)
Stop.
          (HARRY doesn't really hear her. AMINA pulls away from
          under him)
Please stop.
          (she dresses herself)

                    HARRY
What's the matter? Did I hurt you?

                    AMINA
No.

                    HARRY
What is it?

                    AMINA
I…can't…do that.

HARRY

Oh, geez. I'm sorry…did you think I…? I lost my head.

AMINA

No, no, no…it's just…I wanted you to know. I didn't want you to think I'm refusing you because I don't want to…

HARRY

Refusing me? No, no. It's okay. Really. I understand. I went too far.

AMINA

It may sound so, I don't know, so old fashioned. Naïve. I'm saving myself for marriage.

HARRY

You don't have to explain it to me.

AMINA

I have to explain it to myself. I have to remember what I want. I have to remember I have had dreams of my own. But now everything is just going away so fast.

HARRY

I'm here to help. I do care about you so much.

AMINA

Do you love me?

HARRY

I…yes, of course I do.

AMINA

You hesitated.

HARRY

No. It's just…

AMINA

There is nothing that stinks more than someone who hesitates saying "I love you."

HARRY

I adore you, Amina. You caught me off guard.

AMINA

I can't go on like this. I can't keep acting like I'm the great pillar of strength. I thought I'd do anything to keep it all going. Total and complete self-sacrifice. But why should I keep struggling?
(pause)
If you love me you have to take me out of here. Rescue me.

HARRY

That's not the answer you're looking for.

AMINA

If you want to help me then take me away.

HARRY

Now?

AMINA

I need to get out. It's killing me.

HARRY

You know that's not possible. You can't leave now. What about your father?

AMINA

You're a liar, then! You keep saying you want to help me...you care for me. You *love* me! But when I tell you how to show your love, you say it's not possible!

HARRY

That's not fair.

AMINA

Nothing is fair! What are you saying to me? "Life isn't fair, little selfish Amina! Stop complaining. Be realistic. Stand up! Be strong! Fuck your needs and wants!"

HARRY

I didn't say that.

AMINA

Liar! Your love is worthless to me.

HARRY

I'm here to help you…

AMINA

Would you stop saying that!? You've lived your cushy life away from any real danger. You have no idea what real danger is! No one will help me. It's all hopeless!
> (HARRY attempts to physically comfort her, but she
> pushes him away)

Why won't you save me? Why? Because you're too full of your own pitiful self to really care! Go back to your safe NYU student bubble and I'll stay here in my hell-hole Morocco! Get out of my sight!
> (HARRY starts to walk away)

I'm so sorry! No, don't…please don't go away.
> (HARRY stops)

Hold me. Just…hold me.
> (HARRY goes to her and holds her)

Baba! My poor Baba! I'm so sorry. I'm so scared.
> (She weeps in his arms. LIGHTS DOWN)

ACT 2 SCENE 3

Nadir's office, next day. JAMILA comes into the office using a
key to enter, with a small gift wrapped and a bottle of wine. It is
the two-year anniversary of their getting together. She is all
dolled up and she comes in looking for Nadir.

JAMILA

Nadir?
>(She doesn't get an answer. She looks for something in
>her purse, can't find it, then starts looking in drawers in
>Nadir's desk. Finds what she is looking for, a COMB, but
>then seems puzzled about pictures on his desk and holds
>them up to examine them. She looks upset at what she
>sees. NADIR sees the door is open and comes in
>suddenly as she puts them down as if she hasn't looked at
>them)

NADIR

That's a pretty outfit.

JAMILA
>(moves to her gift and wine bottle)

I couldn't find my comb so I was looking for one in your desk.

NADIR

And you found what you were looking for?

JAMILA
>(holds it up)

Here. Oh. Happy two-year anniversary.
>(picks up gift and bottle and brings it to NADIR)

For you.
>(hands him gift)

And for celebrating.
>(holds up bottle)

NADIR
(goes to desk and puts down the gift)
This is for later. What I'd like you to do now is give me your
opinion.

JAMILA

About what?

NADIR

Faiza. Rachid Kahlil's 14-year-old daughter. You know her,
don't you?

JAMILA

Yes.

NADIR

Well, Rachid tells me she wants very badly to be an actress.

JAMILA

Oh.

NADIR

I had Bandar take some photographs of her, to see if she is
photogenic for the screen.
(takes photos to JAMILA)
Do you think she is pretty?

JAMILA

I suppose.

NADIR

I think she is a rare beauty. We will have to test her to see if she
has talent, of course. I'll be bringing her in to my office…to test
her. I think she will do very well, don't you?

JAMILA

I don't know.

NADIR

She reminds me of a younger, untouched you. Untouched by…things in life. She *is* stunning, isn't she?
(JAMILA doesn't answer, but combs her hair into a mirror)
Exquisite. Like the Ahmed virgins at this age.

JAMILA

Why do you keep calling them that? What makes you so sure they are still virgins?

NADIR

You worked in the Ahmed Theatre. You know what they are like.

JAMILA

Is that what is so appealing about them to you?

NADIR

Appealing? Just like that American boy Amina brought back is to you?

JAMILA

He's different from the men here. That's very appealing.

NADIR

Has he made *you* any offers?
(JAMILA is silent)
I didn't think so. Amina will find a real man for herself here in Morocco.

JAMILA

You talk so much about her, I think you'd like to get her for yourself.

NADIR

She's just a diva, Jamila. She is nothing. Now this one…
(holds up the photo of Faiza)
This one's barely ripe off the tree, but she looks very promising.
(puts photo down)
But that's enough about business.
(moves to JAMILA but she moves to her bag)

75

JAMILA

Actually, I have a bit of business.

NADIR

And what is that?

JAMILA

A rumor I heard.

NADIR

You shouldn't repeat rumors. They are usually untrue.

JAMILA

This one was about an attempted kidnapping that was prevented.

NADIR

Kidnapping? And where did you hear such a thing?

JAMILA

Is it true?

NADIR

Is what true?

JAMILA

That you were part of a kidnapping attempt to take Amina Ahmed from the airport?

NADIR

You're walking a dangerous path, here. Be very careful.

JAMILA

Were you?

NADIR

No, I was not part of anything of the sort and that is a rumor I would suggest you don't repeat.

JAMILA

There was a plan, wasn't there? To take Amina. But Abbas stopped it from happening because he went to the airport. They wouldn't dare do anything if he…

NADIR

(suddenly shouting)
Jamila!
(she stops, as he now speaks calmly)
I would suggest you forget what you think you know.

JAMILA

What is the truth?

NADIR

What do you care about them? What did they do for you? Abbas never made you a star, as I have. You owe them nothing.

JAMILA

(goes to the desk and picks up the pictures of Faiza)
If you want to dump me now that I am older and fuck a 14-year old girl with her father's permission in return for a government job, that's one thing. I'll deal with that. But if you were going to let Amina be…hurt…because you hate her father…that's something I can't live with.

NADIR

(sweetly)
Jamila, you have worked yourself up over nothing. There was no plan to kidnap anyone. Your jealousy of Amina and now Faiza has got to stop.
(goes to her and starts to stroke her)
You have to believe me.
(kissing her, she resists, but only slightly)
You are so beautiful, Jamila. You are my gem. And…
(goes to his desk and pulls out a wrapped box and gives it
to JAMILA. She reluctantly takes it)
…do you think you are the only one who has an anniversary gift today. Open it.

NADIR (Cont'd)
(she does. It is a real 24 carat gold belt. She is shocked)
Yes, it's very real. Twenty-four carat gold and fifteen thousand
American dollars. Put it on.
(JAMILA starts to, but NADIR takes it from her and puts it
around her from behind her in an embrace)

JAMILA
It's beautiful. It's like a wedding gift.
(NADIR moves from her, taking the bottle of wine, then
goes to the door and locks it)

NADIR
More than that. It shows what great value you have for me.
Does it not?

JAMILA
Yes.

NADIR
Will you stop your jealous rages, then? They have no
foundation. Now...let's celebrate.
(NADIR strokes her affectionately, kisses her
passionately, then takes her hand and gently leads her
out of the offices into another room where it is obvious
they will be having relations. LIGHTS DOWN)

ACT 2 SCENE 4

Ahmed home, sunset. AREEJ is going through books, looking for the one she is going to bring to the hospital to read to her father while he is in his coma. JAMILA comes to the doorway.

JAMILA

Areej?
> (AREEJ wheels around, dropping the book she had)

AREEJ

Oh, Jamila! If I had a gun you'd be dead right now.

JAMILA

That bad?

AREEJ

Yes, it is.

JAMILA

I didn't mean to frighten you! The door was wide open.

AREEJ
> (goes back to looking at the books)

I left it open for air. It's so stuffy. Everything is making it hard for me to breath.

JAMILA

I understand.

AREEJ

I doubt it. You have plenty of clear air to breath up in your penthouse.

JAMILA

It's not a penthouse. It's just an apartment.

AREEJ

It's better than this.

JAMILA

You may not believe it, but I loved all the time I spent with your family, here. It was some of the best years of my life.

AREEJ

Well, whatever. You came here for a reason? Because I want to go and read to my father. He's read a book every day of his life. It isn't going to stop now, if I can help it.

JAMILA

I'm looking for Amina. I was going to phone but I thought she might ignore my call.

AREEJ

Why do you want her?

JAMILA

It's private.

AREEJ

Really? Well, she's with her boyfriend, the dashing Mr. Zilch, planning their escape to America.

JAMILA

Amina is leaving?

AREEJ

Looks like it. They've, you know, fallen in love. She's leaving. It's final.

JAMILA

But you're going away, too? To Egypt?

AREEJ

My plans were made before theirs. I don't know what to do but get money from somewhere. I'm useless here. Tariq and Shama will live at our house and keep tabs on my father. He'll let us know what is happening. It's no use staying here and just waiting.

(has finally picked out the book she wants, and moves to her bag and phone)

JAMILA

Wait, Areej. Areej...I...I'm so sorry about Abbas.

AREEJ

Yeah, thanks.

JAMILA

No, I really mean it. When you took me in, he was like a father to...

AREEJ

Save it for the camera. You only made trouble for us. My father was accused of all kinds of things when you were with us. Can you just erase what you did?

JAMILA

It wasn't my fault. What they thought. There was never anything between us. I swear.

AREEJ

We knew that. But no one else did. My father treated you with respect even if you didn't treat yourself that way. He was repaid for his kindness with misery.

JAMILA

I've changed.
        (AREEJ laughs)
Do you remember the play we did where I was the 16-year-old daughter, and I had to pull a gun on the government official because he was going to beat my father, and my mother stops me? Your mother was playing another character, so even though Amina was the same age as me, she had to play my mother. She was so angry. She felt like she was already being told she was old and unattractive.

AREEJ

What about it?

JAMILA

She refused. But then your father told her there would be many women whose beauty would fade even younger than she was. Hers would stay radiant because she was shining from the inside out. You know what I thought? I said, to myself, "Jamila, you are ugly on the inside, so that's all that will shine through you. Ugliness."

AREEJ

I'm sorry. That's not true.

JAMILA

Really? You and your sister have made it clear to me over and over.

AREEJ

Then I'm ashamed of myself.

JAMILA

We all had dreams. To be stars. Shining little divas. But you and Amina have a real light inside. I don't.

AREEJ

That's…It's just not true.

JAMILA

If you knew all the darkness I have to deal with inside me. Everything I do is an act. I'm a great actress because I fool everyone. Even you. But not now. Not anymore.
	(takes AREEJ by both arms)
They were going to kidnap Amina.

AREEJ

Who was?

JAMILA

I'm not exactly sure. It was a plot of some kind to kidnap her at the airport.

                          AREEJ
Wait. What? This is…why?

                          JAMILA
Revenge. Your father has a million enemies or haven't you
noticed?

                          AREEJ
But why pick Amina? Why not me?

                          JAMILA
She was vulnerable at the airport. And if they wanted to teach
Abbas a lesson…if they took Amina and…did something to
her…that would be punishment enough.

                          AREEJ
So, that's why my father was afraid. He knew all about it. Amina
should never know this. Swear you'll never say it to her.

                          JAMILA
She has a right to know. Who to blame.

                          AREEJ
Nadir? Bastard!

                          JAMILA
I don't know if he knew about it at the time but I'm sure he knows
now. And he'll do nothing about it.

                          AREEJ
You continue to stay with him! That bastard who knew! Is this
kidnap attempt why you wanted to talk with Amina?

                          JAMILA
No, it's something else.

                          AREEJ
Don't tell her. Swear!

JAMILA

Okay, I swear.

AREEJ

Is she still in danger? Are we?

JAMILA

I'm not sure.

AREEJ

I have to go. I have to think...
            (taking her phone and bag with the book, starts to exit)

JAMILA

Do you know where Amina is?

AREEJ

One of the cafés or bars, near the hospital, I think. They went to celebrate...or drink themselves into amnesia. Come with me.

(JAMILA exits with AREEJ. LIGHTS DOWN)

ACT 2 SCENE 5

Café/Bar in Casablanca which serves alcoholic beverages, same evening. AMINA has been drinking more than HARRY, so she is tipsy.

                    AMINA
But I didn't *know*!

                    HARRY
But I did.

                    AMINA
It was so fast! How could you know?

                    HARRY
It's like when you see a screen star and you can't your eyes off her. That was me with you.

                    AMINA
That's infatuation. I'm talking about love. How do you know you love me?

                    HARRY
I don't know how I know. I just know.

                    AMINA
It feels so different. This.

                    HARRY
Than what?

                    AMINA
Than all the crushes I've had all my life. I'd wake up and whoosh! Feelings all gone. But you. I hated you at first. You were so rude. So cocky.

HARRY
That's how real love works. First you hate them, then you fall madly in love with them, then it settles down to a livable roar.

AMINA
I'm in love with you and I hope it never settles down.

HARRY
It has to. You can't sustain that.

AMINA
Yes, you can. It's like in Casablanca, at that terrible moment when Ilsa lets Rick convince her to go with Victor. Mr. Sensible. It was supposed to be her and *Rick* on that plane. They screwed up! But now we are making it right. Ilsa and Rick high and mighty in love and getting on that plane!
    (she clinks her drink and they drink)

HARRY
Really, no matter which way it ended, it was still a story written just to manipulate the audience.

AMINA
Just like we manipulate our story, huh? Like movies. Like songs. Like the song they used in that movie, "Amelie"....
    (sings the song, "Si tu n'etais pas la")
"Si tu n'etais pas la
Comment pourrais-je vivre
Je ne connaitrais pas
Ce bonheur qui m'enivre
    (speaks these words as she dances around him)
If you weren't there
How could I live?
I wouldn't know
This exhilarating happiness
    (sings, putting herself in his arms)
Quand je suis dans tes bras

AMINA (Cont'd)

(speaks)
My cheerful heart surrenders
How could I live
If you weren't there?
(she spins him in a dance with a big ending)
It's Fréhel's song. Do you know her? During the Second World
War she was a wonderful singer. So emotional and fragile.
She's the only French thing I love.

HARRY

(seriously)
And you're the only Moroccan thing I love. I do, Amina.

AMINA

Then why are we still here?
(sings from "West Side Story")
"I like to be in America
Okay by me in America!"

HARRY

Amina? Who is going to tell your father?

AMINA

Oh, Harrison, don't.

HARRY

I know he's in the coma but maybe he's conscious. There are a
lot of stories about people being in comas and yet they know
everything that's happened to them.

AMINA

Why are you torturing me?

HARRY

I want his blessing.

AMINA

I give you mine. Isn't that enough?

87

HARRY

There is something about it all that doesn't seem like you.

AMINA

If you don't like me, then hate me so you can love me all the more.

HARRY

I'm serious.

AMINA

I'm tired of fighting. You still don't get the danger here, do you?

HARRY

I guess I don't.
        (JAMILA enters and AMINA sees her)

AMINA

        (in Arabic)
How did you find us? What do you want?

JAMILA

Areej said you'd be here. I've come on friendly terms. To talk.

AMINA

Friendly terms? To talk about what?

JAMILA

Privately.

HARRY

Hello Jamila. I'm sorry I never thanked you for helping me find Amina.

JAMILA

You're welcome.

AMINA

No, you're not! Keep your greedy paws off! Watch out! She'll draw you in like a butterfly and then bite you like snake.

HARRY

Give her a chance.

AMINA

I've heard enough from her for many years. She made life hell for my father when he was kind to her. She's made her choices. She's slept in her bed. Now let her make it.

HARRY

You have that backwards.

JAMILA

I just need help and I don't…I don't have anyone else to turn to.

AMINA

You turn to me for help? That's some joke.

HARRY

She's a little drunk. Maybe this isn't the best time.

JAMILA

She might take what I have to say better drunk. I wish I was. I wish I was dead and buried.

HARRY

This doesn't sound like the Jamila I met at the station.

AMINA

You mean the hot tamale? We don't have to go into details, do we?

JAMILA

Okay. C'est ma honte terrible. I'm nothing. I'll go.
        (starts to exit)

HARRY

Jamila, wait.
        (takes her by the arm)
Amina. Please let her talk.

JAMILA

She's right. I am a snake. Cut off my head and be done with it.

HARRY

Amina.

AMINA

I don't know. My head is starting to pound.

HARRY

I'll get you coffee.

AMINA

No. I'll be fine. Alright. Jamila, I'll listen to you.

JAMILA

Thank you. Can we go someplace private?

AMINA

Let's go home.

JAMILA

No! Very private.

AMINA

Let's go to the Ahmed Theatre. I have the key.

HARRY

I'll walk you there. It's getting late.

AMINA

With us on either arm, we'll look like street walkers. Better we go alone.

HARRY

Call me when you're done and I'll come get you.

AMINA

We'll be alright.

(they kiss, and HARRY starts to pull away, but AMINA
pulls him back and kisses him very passionately and he's
the one who pulls away. JAMILA exits with AMINA,
helping her a bit as she is tipsy)

                    HARRY
          (aloud and to himself)
Hell was life without you, my love. Now I've found heaven is *in
hell*.
          (he exits in the opposite direction. LIGHTS DOWN)

ACT 2 SCENE 6

The abandoned Ahmed Theatre, same evening. AMINA unlocks the door and opens curtains to let in streetlight from outside, so they are in semidarkness, with light streaming in.

JAMILA

This is the only place in my life I've ever felt freed from everything.

AMINA

Me too.

JAMILA

Inside the plays we did with all the political corruption there was always a family that loved each other somewhere in there.

AMINA

Yes, he managed to find those moments and make them stand out.
(holds her head)
Jamila, I'm sorry, but my head is starting to really ache. I think I did drink too much. What is it? What's so important?

JAMILA

Remember Rachid Kahlil? He played all the dashing young hypocrites in your father's plays.

AMINA

Of course, I do.

JAMILA

Well, he's been promised a cushy government job by Nadir.

AMINA

How unfortunate for him. I hope he's ready to kiss many asses on the way up to total "Assdom." But what has he done to get it? There's always a price?

JAMILA

He's got a fourteen-year-old daughter, Faiza. You've seen her?
(long pause)

AMINA

He's not...oh, no, no, no. He's not...

JAMILA

Not yet. The payment is Faiza's going to be a big star. Nadir is going to see to it. After he's given her a "screen test" in his office.

AMINA

Oh, God, Jamila. I'm so sorry. But that's the kind of man...the kind government this man is connected to. You jumped right in with both your eyes open. You knew from the start...

JAMILA

Don't tell me what I knew!!! You know nothing about who I am!
(pause)
I'm leaving Nadir and I need your help.

AMINA

How can I help? I can't just hide you in a closet. I have no money to get you out of the country.

JAMILA

No, not like that. I can't help myself. It's inside me.

AMINA

I don't understand.

JAMILA

I never felt I had any control over anything in my life. I just obeyed. In this...I had a choice. It felt good. I wanted to feel good about myself and this felt... good and I didn't want it to stop. But then I became someone else. It wasn't me. It was someone I hated.

AMINA
What are you trying to say?

JAMILA
Nadir isn't the first. My father's brother initiated me. He was 30 and I was 13.
>(laughs)

It was a slow process. He started telling me how gorgeous I was and how I would make a magnificent actress. He'd kiss me a lot. It made me uncomfortable, but then again, it made me excited, too. I loved all the attention. Then he'd take me on little trips. We'd be alone a lot. He was so much fun and so gentle. At some point he'd start to touch me under my clothes and put a finger in private places. At first, I froze, but then he'd whisper the most wonderful things into my ear. I'd relax. And it was fun.

AMINA
You don't have to tell me this.

JAMILA
If I don't I'll go crazy. Please.
>(pause)

Sometimes he'd take my hands and put them on him and he'd pump and pump and...he'd say how special I was to make him feel so wonderful. He made me feel sexy. So desirable. Somehow, I knew this was a lie, but I wanted it to be true. He started laying on top of me and taking it out and pushing up against me. We'd be in the grass and I'd look up and see the beautiful sky and clouds and hear him moaning with satisfaction and I'd think I was a goddess giving him life.

AMINA
Jamila…

JAMILA
Shhhh….I want to tell it. I knew about how real sex was putting it inside, so one day I just opened up and led him into me. He was surprised and didn't want to, but I insisted. It hurt at first, but then, I don't know. I was transported to another place. And he was so kind and gentle. He never forced himself on me.

JAMILA (Cont'd)

(pause)

I started wanting to see him more. I was obsessed, you know.
He'd always bring me gifts and then we'd do it and I was
ravenous. I couldn't stop. This went on for nearly a year. And
then something funny happened. He moved away. Just like
that. My mother said he got a job in Agadir and that was that. I
went crazy.

(pause)

I kept trying to attract older men. I kept trying and failing. Then
my mother found out…I don't know how...and there was a huge
fight with my father. My mother left with me to live with her friend
in Fez. I ran away the week before I turned 16.

AMINA

My father said he found you at the train station in Marrakesh
looking scared and hungry.

JAMILA

That's as far as my money took me. He never told you I was
trying to sell myself to him?

AMINA

He never said a word. We never knew anything and we never
asked. He brought you home and that was all.

JAMILA

When I met Nadir, he reminded me of my uncle. He can be so
kind and gentle when he wants to be. He looked at me the way
my uncle did and I was hooked. It's all inside me…this...and no
matter how I've tried to hide it, it explodes and I'm just a whore.

AMINA

You're not a whore.

JAMILA

What would you call it? Do I do it for money? Position?
Comfort? I do it because I can't stop. I'll leave Nadir and have
nothing, and I'm willing to, to stop this. But I need help.

AMINA

I'm not a therapist!

JAMILA

You are the only person I can trust.

AMINA

But I'm leaving with Harrison!

JAMILA

I don't understand how you can with your father at…

AMINA

It's hopeless with my father in a coma.

JAMILA

But he's still alive.

AMINA

And I'm leaving so I can stay alive!

JAMILA

I've known you to be the bravest…the strongest…the most powerful woman I have ever met. What are you doing, Amina?

AMINA

I don't know. I don't know.

(LIGHTS DOWN)

ACT 2 SCENE 7

Nadir's Office, very late, same night. AMINA is banging on his door. She yells through the shut door.

AMINA
I can see a light. I know you're in there.

> (NADIR comes out from another room, and answers the door)

NADIR
What are you doing here? It's almost midnight.

AMINA
Jamila said you'd be here late. That you had certain business…a rendezvous…you were not likely to miss.

NADIR
And what else did Jamila say?

AMINA
You're dumping her for a fourteen-year-old.

NADIR
She's really delusional.

AMINA
Faiza Kahlil, *for certain favors*, will be an actress for the ministry. Also, her father gets a job. Nice packaged deal. Evil bastard!

NADIR
That's funny.

AMINA
What could possibly be funny?

NADIR
Because, you see, I'm one of the rare *good* ones, Amina. I'm a *good* man. My wife has beautiful clothes. A beautiful house.

NADIR (Cont'd)

She does what she likes. Spends what she likes. My son goes to a wonderful private school with rich friends who love him. They want for *nothing*. And I give Jamila what she wants. How am I an evil bastard? They are all content.

AMINA

Are they? How would you really know?

NADIR

I have always given people just what they *desired*. Jamila more than anyone. Did she show you the belt I gave her? It cost me a fortune, but I wanted her to be happy.

AMINA

That's the kind of gift a man gives his fiancée.

NADIR

Jamila doesn't desire a fiancée! She desires a lover. We have that in common.

AMINA

It's a bribe to keep her content while you embrace your new infatuation, Faiza. You're taking advantage of that little girl's innocence. Her dreams.

NADIR

I'm helping her *fulfill* her dreams!

AMINA

Jamila is leaving you.

NADIR

She is free to do what she likes. See? I'm the good one, once again.

AMINA

She is afraid of you.
> (she holds her head and sits)

NADIR

I'd suggest you go home and…wait. Do I smell liquor?
(stands in front of her)
This is not the perfect Ahmed saint I know.
(close)
I could already see how magnificent you would be when you
were only ten. You lit up that stage like a lightning bolt.
(touches her face, but she moves away)

AMINA

This is not about me. I just…I came to tell you Jamila is leaving
you and I'm helping her and you can't stop her. Then I'm leaving
with Harrison and getting out of here.

NADIR

I really hate that you chose your American puppy over me. I
hope he can keep you satisfied.
(AMINA turns to go)
You know, I can't get over you delusional Ahmeds! You march
into a room, make your pronouncements as if you're on a stage
and then march out and think you're victorious.
(AMINA is at the door)
Like your father showing up at the airport thinking he could
protect you like some mighty god. He scared them away for
now, but it won't always be that easy. Your father has many
enemies.

AMINA

What are you saying about the airport?

NADIR

You don't…oh, so Jamila didn't tell you?

AMINA

What?

NADIR

My sweet. You were going to be kidnapped.
(AMINA is shocked)

NADIR (Cont'd)

Oh, Amina. Let's lay down our weapons and make peace or you'll spend the rest of your days looking over your shoulder wondering not *if* it will happen, but *when*. Don't you realize I'm your only real protection? I'm the *good* one.

(AMINA stands motionless. LIGHTS DOWN)

ACT 2 SCENE 8

Ahmed Home, next morning. Amina is home alone anxiously waiting for Harry to return from making preparations for their departure.

AMINA
Thank God you're back. You left early this morning.

HARRY
I had a lot to do.
          (holds up plane tickets and papers)
There is more to arrange, but so far, we can leave in 4 days if everything else goes smoothly.

AMINA
I got in so late after I spoke with Jamila. I know I was supposed to call you.

HARRY
You're a big girl. I trust you can take care of yourself. And you were with Jamila. The two of you could fight off a lion. So, did she get off her chest whatever it was that was so important?

AMINA
Yes.

HARRY
Was it really that urgent?

AMINA
She's leaving Nadir.

HARRY
Really? Good for her! The Moroccan women are now waking up and staging a revolt.

AMINA

With the Ahmeds as the instigators. Don't be so happy. She's going to lose everything.

HARRY

What is she going to do?

AMINA

We're not sure. I'm going to help her.

HARRY

That's very noble of you, but you're a little occupied right now.

AMINA

Don't dictate to me what I'm doing!

HARRY

I'm not. Just making an observation.

AMINA

Well, you've observed wrong. I'm staying here at least until I can figure out how to keep her safe.

HARRY

She can live with Tariq and Shama, here, when you're gone. There's room.

AMINA

It's too dangerous. And too humiliating.

HARRY

Why humiliating?

AMINA

She needs me. I am the only one she can trust.

HARRY

And you're the only one I love! I don't like competition.

AMINA

It's complicated.

HARRY

You have three days.

AMINA

How dare you tell me what to do!?

HARRY

How dare you ruin our lives with this!

AMINA

Ruin who's life? How selfish of you!

HARRY

How selfish of you! What about me and how I feel? There's danger here for you. You've said so again and again.

AMINA

Mortal danger, yes.

HARRY

Then what are you doing?

AMINA

What I think is right, just as my father would have done.

HARRY

Your father wants you away from here. He told me so, himself, at the hospital. He gave me a new name, Munjid. That means…

AMINA

I know what it means.

HARRY

Your father told me to rescue you.

AMINA

I don't need rescuing.

105

HARRY

That's definitely not the way you made it seem to me.

AMINA

I can't just leave now. And I was drunk. I was…

HARRY

In love. Or so I thought. Now look at you. Who do you think you are?

AMINA

The daughter of Abbas Ahmed, the revolutionary! What do you know about being a revolutionary, *Zilch*?

HARRY

I don't think anyone has ever hurt me as much as you have at this moment.

AMINA

That was so cruel. I'm so sorry. Don't you know what a mixed-up mess you've fallen in love with? I'm so confused. I can't take this anymore.
        (HARRY moves to her)
They were going to kidnap me at the airport when I came home. Nadir knew about it. My father was acting so strange. He came to prevent it. Who knows what they were planning to do? Revenge on my father through hurting me.

HARRY

Oh, God, Amina. That's it. You're coming with me or we're done. I'm serious. If you love me you will be on that plane with me.

AMINA

I will not be given an ultimatum to prove my love!

HARRY

Then say good-bye to me right now. I can't stand the pain watching you struggling everyday trying to find yourself. I found you. You are found, Amina. There is no more searching!
> (AREEJ suddenly walks in and stops, sits and says nothing)

AMINA

Areej?
> (silence as AREEJ seems in a stupor)

Areej? What is it?

AREEJ

> (quietly, matter of fact)

I was reading him his favorite play. Brecht's "Galileo." I was at the last scene where the children sing and Andrea is sneaking out Galileo's famous book, and I thought I heard him say my name. So, I got closer. He did say something but I couldn't understand it. He was coming out of the coma! He was alive again! He said in a very clear voice "I can see you, Amira. I can see you!" And then…then, he was gone.
> (pause)

Baba is gone.

> (AMINA goes to her but she puts out her hand to leave her alone and exits. AMINA and HARRY are stunned. AMINA runs to HARRY and they embrace. LIGHTS DOWN)

ACT 2 SCENE 9

Casablanca Airport, one week later. HARRY and AMINA are standing in an embrace at the gate with two pieces of luggage. They stay in this embrace for a moment, then pull back looking at one another.

AMINA

I'm sorry, sir, I didn't catch your name.

HARRY

It is…
     (HARRY kisses her passionately)

AMINA

I'm not quite getting it. Must be the accent.
     (HARRY bends her backwards and kisses her in an
     exaggerated style, then lifts her back up)
Hmmmm. Still can't make it out.

HARRY

We're drawing a crowd.

AMINA

You've forgotten I'm famous? They'll be running up soon for an autograph.

HARRY

I'll protect you.

AMINA

I don't want protection from that! Where is Areej?

HARRY

She said she had to get something she wanted you to have.

AMINA

I don't need anything now.
     (hangs on HARRY)

HARRY

Something your father gave her.
>(AMINA lets him go, becomes serious)

AMINA

Oh. She shouldn't do that. He gave it to her. She should keep it.

HARRY

There must have been hundreds of people at your father's memorial. What were they saying when they went up to pay their respects?

AMINA

>(in Arabic)

Thank you, Munjid.
>(in English)

Thank you, Rescuer. It was one of his favorite characters he'd play. He was the bumbling knight-type, coming in to help people, but always failing miserably.

HARRY

He named me Munjid, after that character, didn't he?

AMINA

He always had keen insight into people. He pegged you right the minute he met you.

HARRY

There were a lot of people at my father's wake I didn't know. They all came up to me but I don't remember anything they said. All their faces were a blur. One of them gave me a medal my father won in high school for something. It was really nothing, but when he gave it to me, I started to bawl like crazy. That was a good thing. That opened me up and let out the flood inside. Then I was okay. Maybe Areej's gift will do the same for you.

AMINA

If I'm ever opened up like that nothing will stop the flood in me.

(AREEJ and JAMILA arrive. AREEJ is pulling a small carryon bag)

AREEJ

Sorry we took so long. I wanted it wrapped.
(hands AMINA a small box. AMINA starts to unwrap it)
No, no, not now! Later. When you're alone.
(AMINA puts it away)

AMINA

I thought when you said you had a surprise for me it was that you were going to dye your hair back to its original color.

AREEJ

You still hate it that much?

AMINA

No. I love you this much.
(AMINA embraces AREEJ)

JAMILA

(to HARRY)
You will be missed, homme délicieux!

AREEJ

I don't like good-byes, so let's just get this over with.
(AMINA and AREEJ hug and HARRY and JAMILA hug)

JAMILA

I'll take good care of Amina, I swear. We'll stay safe. We hired Tariq as our bodyguard.

HARRY

Oh, that makes me feel so much better.

JAMILA

Tomorrow is the meeting with Nadir and the staff at the TV Station. I think they might consider giving us that third season

JAMILA (Cont'd)

after all. And we're opening the old Ahmed Theatre to do children's theatre, like Amina and I used to do as children. Things are going to happen fast.

HARRY

We'll come back fast.

AREEJ

With oodles of cash, too. I promise. I'll do my marvelous Rita Hayworth imitation and they'll be falling to their knees on Broadway.

JAMILA

Falling to their knees with laughter.

AREEJ

Jamila! Well, Cairo wasn't ready for me yet, anyway.

AMINA

Neither is New York! Please keep your eye on her, Harrison.

HARRY

No. My eye is on you. And will be until we return.

AREEJ

I'm going to make them beg to give us money. Harrison has friends in high places.

HARRY

More like Brooklyn Heights. But it looks promising.

AMINA

Please can I have one more…
       (HARRY before she can finish embraces her and they kiss
       a long time)

JAMILA

Just like in the movies.

AREEJ

Yes, but his is a zombie movie and I'm really the walking dead.
>   (She slaps HARRY on the back and he lets go of AMINA)

Come on, chaperone! Before you change your mind.
>   (HARRY mouths, *I love you.* to AMINA and she does the
>   same to him)

AREEJ

For Baba.

AMINA

For Baba.

>   (HARRY takes two pieces of luggage and AREEJ takes
>   one and they exit while AMINA and JAMILA stand
>   watching them, then they slowly exit in the opposite
>   direction. LIGHTS DOWN)

END OF PLAY

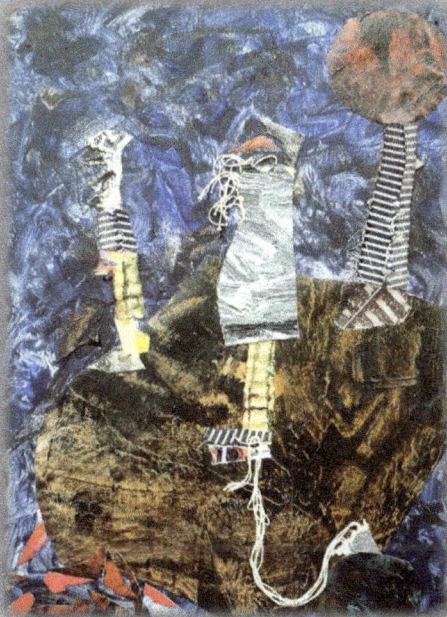

for more information

contact

karenklami@gmail.com

www.ingramcontent.com/pod-product-compliance
Lightning Source LLC
Chambersburg PA
CBHW072201090426
42740CB00012B/2339